SEVEN
LEGENDARY
MONSTERS

SEVEN
LEGENDARY
MONSTERS

CLARA ELENA GARCÍA

MONRISE

Copyright © 2025 Clara Elena García

All rights reserved. No part of this book may be reprinted or reproduced or utilised in any form or by any electronic, mechanical, or other means, now known or hereafter invented, including photocopying and recording, or in any information storage or retrieval system, without permission in writing from the publisher.

Paperback 978-0-6459852-8-3
eBook 978-1-7640782-2-1

Editor
Wallea Eaglehawk

Copy editors
Emma Mitchell
Pooja Kumar

Cover art and design by Oz Montania

First published in 2025

Moonrise
Wonnarua and Gubbi Gubbi Country, Australia
www.moonrise.revolutionaries.com.au

*Che Paraguay porã,
mi corazón siempre
está contigo*

CONTENTS

Author's Note 11
Monsters Family Tree 14
Prologue: On Gods and Monsters 15

Chapter 1: Keraná 21
    Tupã 22
    Rupave 24
    Sypave 28
    Taú 30
    Angatupyry 40
    Arasy 44
    Añaretãsy 50
    Pokõi 54

Chapter 2: Teju Jagua 57
    Teju Jagua 58
    Fruit and Honey 62
    Lizard Brain 64
    On Curses 68
    Caña y Miel 70
    Buried Treasure 73
    Cave of the Heart 78

Chapter 3: Mbói Tu'ĩ 83
    Mbói Tu'ĩ 84
    Squawk 86
    Vare'a 89
    Taruba 92
    Naipi 95
    Iguazú 99
    Arko Iris 102

Chapter 4: Moñái 107
    Moñái 108
    Antennae 111
    Plumas 113
    Prankster 116
    Ribcage 118
    Horned Serpent 120
    Loot 122

Chapter 5: Jasy Jateré 125
    Jasy Jateré 126
    The Child 129
    Jasy's Song 131
    Siesta 133
    Mita'i 135
    Silbato 139
    Solitude 141

Chapter 6: Kurupí **145**
    Kurupí 146
    Pyhare 149
    Sacred Serpent 154
    Divining Rod 158
    Tatakua 161
    Vessel 163
    Kuña Mbareté 169

Chapter 7: Ao Ao **175**
    Ao Ao 176
    Untamed 181
    Ka'aguy 184
    Pindovy 187
    Hearts of Palm 189
    Ao 191
    Yvyty 194

Chapter 8: Luisón **197**
    Luisón 198
    Werewolf 201
    Lunar Eclipse 206
    Seventh Son 208
    Shapeshifter 211
    Cementerio 213
    On Death 215

Chapter 9: Porãsy 219
    Porãsy 220
    Tumé Arandú 224
    Jahari Gua'a 227
    Ka'a Ruvicha 230
    Temikuave'e 234
    Ñemendápe 238
    Ko'Êtĩ 241
    Py'aguasú 245
    Mbyja Ko'ê 249

Epilogue: On Monsters and Men 253

Compendium of Mortals and Monsters 257
    The Monsters 259
    The Mortals 272

Glossary of Guaraní Terms 283

References 285

About the Author 287

AUTHOR'S NOTE

Paraguay is a tiny landlocked country in the heart of South America that is bordered by Argentina to the southwest, Brazil to the northeast, and Bolivia to the northwest. Prior to the conquest by the Spanish in the 1500s, Paraguay was home to a number of indigenous tribes belonging to the Guaraní people. Although their demographic dominance of the region has been reduced by European colonization, there are still contemporary Guaraní populations in Paraguay to this day.

In modern day Paraguay, the Seven Legendary Monsters are considered primary figures in Guaraní mythology. While several of the lesser deities, or even the original humans, are forgotten in the verbal tradition of some areas, the Seven are still a large part of what makes up Paraguayan culture, particularly in the countryside where they are still spoken of as more than mere superstition.

The myths and legends of the Guaraní were passed down predominantly through oral storytelling traditions. Over time, European influences and the erasure of indigenous knowledge have shaped these myths into the whimsical stories that they are today. Most notably, the tales were reimagined by Paraguayan poet Rosicrán in the 1920s and reshaped into the commonly known version that is the Guaraní creation myth that follows.

As a result, many of these stories have been watered down and distilled into cautionary tales told to Paraguayan children, similar to Aesop's Fables. While the roots of these stories may not be commonly known, the morals, values and common themes of these tales persist within Paraguayan culture to this day.

If you ask a Paraguayan if they believe in the Seven, they will most likely shrug but then tell you a story about their own encounter with one of these beings, or that of someone they know. It could be a shadow seen in the forest, or a flock of birds in the open fields, or a whistle in the night that poses the question—what if these monsters are more than just fables?

The way these myths and legends have endured in the psyche of the Paraguayan people speaks

AUTHOR'S NOTE

to their desire to keep alive the magic of their ancestors and their deep connection with the natural world.

While the origins of the stories may be deeply buried, the struggle between the forces of good and evil lives on in the hearts and minds of all who believe in the Seven Legendary Monsters.

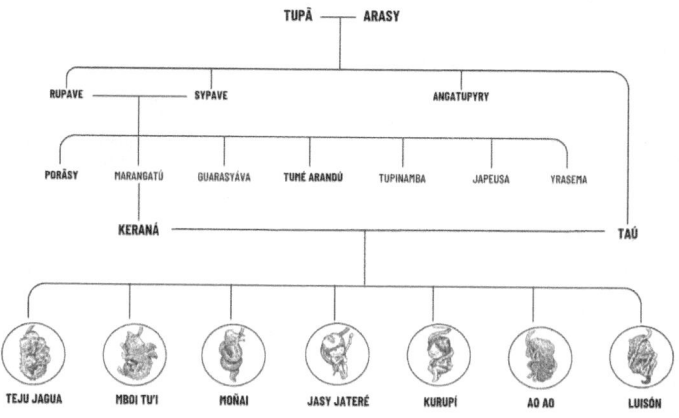

PROLOGUE

On Gods and Monsters

The Guaraní Creation Myth
Inspired by the Paraguayan poet, Rosicrán

The primary figure in most Guarani creation myths is *Tupã*, the supreme deity of all creation. With the help of the celestial mother *Arasy*, *Tupã* descended upon the Earth on a hill in the region of Aregúa, Paraguay. From that location, he created all that is found upon the face of the earth, including the rivers, forests, mountains, and the animals.

Tupã then created humanity in an elaborate ceremony, forming clay statues of man and woman using a mixture of various plants and elements from nature, including the rich red Paraguayan soil. After breathing life into the human forms, he left them with the brother spirits of good and evil, *Angatupyry and Taú*, and departed.

SEVEN LEGENDARY MONSTERS

The original humans created by *Tupã* were named *Rupave* and *Sypave*, whose names mean "Father of the people" and "Mother of the people" respectively.

The first of their sons was *Tumé Arandú*, considered to be the wisest of men and the great prophet of the Guaraní people. Second of their sons was *Marangatú*, a benevolent and generous leader of his people, and father of *Keraná*, the mother of the Seven Legendary Monsters. And so our tale begins.

As legend has it, *Taú* became enamored with *Keraná* and tried to lure her away, causing an uproar among the Guaraní. *Angatypyry* intervened and he and *Taú* fought each other for seven days and seven nights until *Taú* was at last overwhelmed and banished from the village.

However, *Taú* would not be so easily defeated. He returned in secret and kidnapped the beautiful *Keraná* as she lay sleeping, making her his wife despite all odds.

As punishment, *Arasy* cursed the couple so that all but one of their children would be born as

PROLOGUE

hideous monsters. After their birth, evil spread across the Earth for seven years.

No one was safe from the monsters. *Kurupí* kidnapped and raped the maidens. *Moñai* stole and looted. *Luisón* ravaged the cemeteries. *Jasy Jateré*, in his pranks, kidnapped children. *Ao Ao* devastated the herds of the tribe, while, with his squawks, *Mbói Tu'i* waited lurking in the jungle. *Teju Jagua's* fiery gaze in the darkness of the caves inspired only more fear and superstition.

Tumê Arandú saw the suffering of his people at the hands of the Seven Legendary Monsters and decided to ask *Tupã* for help. *Tupã* heard the prayer and sent a message to *Tumê Arandú* through *jahari gua'a* (a macaw) that the defeat of the Seven Legendary Monsters can only be carried out by a beautiful maiden.

Tumê Arandú returned home and related what he had heard to his tribe. The youngest and most beautiful of his sisters, *Porãsy*, bravely volunteered to help with the plan, even if it meant sacrificing herself for the good of mankind.

Porãsy's sublime sacrifice to free the land from the cursed monsters will be remembered forever. *Tupã*, to reward her dedication, raised the heroine's soul to heaven and turned it into a small but intense point of light. From that point on, the spirit of *Porãsy* lights up the sky at dusk and dawn.

CHAPTER I
Keraná

Mother of Monsters

TUPÃ

Lovingly sculpted
        from ash
and clay
vine for hair and
tree
        for heart

Rupave
        Sypave
father and
        mother
of all

children of the
earth
        and sky

I gave you form,
now
        how will
you live
this   life

KERANÁ

left alone
with only
good and evil
      by your
side

will you   fly
or will you   fall

will you crash
      and   burn

will you learn
      to love or
learn to   lie

    che memby

my children
what will become
      of you

will you be men
      or will you be

        monstruos

RUPAVE

The fruits
of *paraíso*
      turn to
dust in my
      mouth

as you turn
      your back
on your creations
      and ascend

to   observe
your puppets
from celestial
      throne

to laugh
      at our
transgressions
as we   fail

for that is
our purpose
here on this

KERANÁ

      yvy
is it   not

to learn the
    nature
of our sin
we first must
fall

but why must
mankind
    be the
one to bear
the burden of
    this curse

are we not
    allowed
to take
our pleasure
without
    pain

you leave
us with Taú
    to learn
from wicked

deeds
and Angatupyry
      to temper
our desire

      when
you could
simply leave
us   be

what kind of
parent   does
that to his
child

are we
not born of
your   image
too

what does
that make
you   devil
or   divine

che ru
      my father

KERANÁ

if you are
filled   with
        sin

       then

what

       are we

SYPAVE

The shores
      of *Ypacaraí*
bear witness to
our pain

abandoned
      by celestial
parents too
creídos to care
for   their
own
      children

here   on
hilltop we
can   see the
world they
created
awash with
pluvial
      abundance

this *lago*
is our

KERANÁ

    birthright
and our bounty
but *belleza*
is tempered by
our   dread

alone with
good   and evil
to abide
to learn to
love   or
    learn to lie

for what
other   choices
do we have
when we
have Taú
    by our side

TAÚ

What is love if
not all
       consuming
what is lust if
not my
       destiny

I never meant
her   harm

her innocent
allure   broke down
       even the
       walls of
the hardest heart

who would
have   thought
that the spirit of
evil   could
be capable of
       amor

KERANÁ

but is it evil to desire
or is it just
human
      nature

why should
I not   take what
I am
      owed before
I am denied

she lies asleep
for   dreams
      to claim and
mine are filled with
thoughts of her

she gave me
no   choice
      but to
devour
      her

sweetness of
      honeyed
light on
golden skin

>   the play
>   of *sombras*
> on her lips
>
> the curves
> of hip bones
>   formed like
> the rolling *cerros*
>   that
> surround me
>
> lush with   her
> verdant
>   vegetation
> her valleys
> bursting   with
> fecund
>   possibility
>
> ready and
>   willing
> like   virgin
> earth
> soft and ready
>   to plant
> my flag into
> for
> my conquest

KERANÁ

if love is
an act of
      will
to possess   is
an act
      of war

this blade at your
throat
      is my
way of saying
"I do"

and so I will
steal her
in   her
sleep

a stunning
      trophy
to adorn
      my bed

can you blame
me

        I am
Taú
        I am
no paragon

so
tell me

who in
their right
        mind would
not be tempted

who in
their deepest
        heart would
not fall

if that
makes me
        evil

así

        sea

KERANÁ

If sleep is such a sin
        then am I
        condemned
for all eternity

why do women
always bear the
burden
        for the sins
of evil men

how was I to know that
in slumber my
        innocence
would be ravished

by a wicked spirit
and turned
        against my will
for evil purpose

I never asked
        to become
a legend

SEVEN LEGENDARY MONSTERS

I lived a simpler
        existence
in those days

amongst flowers
and fronds of the
        lapacho I slept
and dreamt of sunlight

not knowing that horror
lurked beyond
        dreamscape
hidden in plain sight

beyond the haunting
        sound of flute
and birdsong lurks
        the truth

like the coat of
yaguareté the
        shadow's
alluring ripples
mask   evil intent

with his   skin
the color of   earth

KERANÁ

he entranced   me

with his   smooth
tongue and
enticing   words
he ensnared   me

with his amber
eyes and
magic   flute
he beguiled   me

awaiting the chance
to stalk in and
       claim me
defile me
burn me to the ground

and leave me as
nothing more than
       a cautionary
tale

cursed now
       forevermore
by my own
mother's   hand

SEVEN LEGENDARY MONSTERS

doomed to   bear
in my womb the
      destruction
of mankind

what did I
do to deserve
      my fate
I've learned
      my lesson

beware the hearts
      of men
and monsters

beware the
      honeyed
tongue

beware my story
      che memby
my children

for the protectors
      of the earth
and   sky

KERANÁ

are always held to
        blame for
mankind's ills

you will learn
        someday

you're not
yet a   mother
you're not
yet a   father

but one day
        you will
be

ANGATUPYRY

My brother
my balance
      my foe

why did he
      have to fall
in lust

what did she
do to change
      him into
someone
I barely
      recognize

      before we
were merely
equals

balanced in
      duality
opposing forces
evil and
      good

KERANÁ

brought to
life   by
Tupã's hand

bound to
teach   the
first of
        man

        now we
are bitter
rivals
fighting for
        redemption

for seven
days and
        seven nights

we fought
to   prove a
point

        that evil
cannot triumph
over good, but

SEVEN LEGENDARY MONSTERS

little did I know that
        banishment
made him bold

as he betrayed
me in   cold
        blood

why must he
always win
        the fight

why can he
not   accept
his loss

        my brother
my balance
        my foe

damned now for
all eternity

and with him
        the very girl
he claimed
        to save

KERANÁ

the lovely Keraná
cursed now
    for his
mistake

Arasy's
wrath borne
fully   by
    her
brood

how did
we get
    here

my brother
my balance
    my foe

ARASY

No one
understands
       a mother's
           curse
no one asks
if the spirits
themselves
       weep
over choices
we are forced
      to make

my   earthly
child, I have
       wronged you

how can I beg for
your
      forgiveness
when it was I who
hurt   you so

his betrayal
forced   my

KERANÁ

hand
        and you
an unwitting
        sacrifice

I intended
        to punish
him, not
        you
can't you
        see

the sins of
        wicked
men left
unpunished
        lead only
to more pain

a necessary
        evil
that we as women
are forced
        to bear

how cold this
distance, how empty

these arms   that
      cannot hold you

what good
the moon's
      gravity if
I cannot cradle
your *corazón* in
      my hands

how do I dry
your tears, *che
membykuña*
      my daughter

how do I go
on living knowing
I have cursed
      you for all
eternity

helplessly
watching sorrow
      stalk in on
silent feet

wrap you

KERANÁ

in   vines that
bind, laced with
honey and
        thorns

shooting
you with *flechas
venenosas*
poison darts
        of blame

seeing men slander
you   for merely
sleeping, for simply
        existing

none of this is
your fault   my
child,   it is my
own burden to
bear
        and   yet

I cannot bear
to see   you   cry

SEVEN LEGENDARY MONSTERS

my only solace is
when you   lift
your tear-stained
face to mine

       and you
remember that

you hold
     la luna
within
your   mind

       and
        la tierra
      within
      your   body

and
    el universo
within
your   soul

child of the
earth and
      sky

KERANÁ

never forget

who
      you
           are

AÑARETÃSY

Ñandejára
what have
    I done

how did
I awake
    from dream

into such
horror, these
    monstruos

that only
lurked in my
    mind's eye

borne in
blood and sweat
    and tears

brought to
life before
    my eyes

KERANÁ

my love
transformed
    into their fear

my dreams
transformed
    into nightmares

my mother's
curse it
    haunts me

giving birth to
ghastly
    forms and

twisted bodies
they must hate
    me, but I am

Añaretãsy
Mother of Monsters
    I know them well

I know there's
more than
    meets the eye

SEVEN LEGENDARY MONSTERS

can you not sense
sadness in
their mournful
    howls

can you not see
the *belleza* under
    beastly skin

can you not hear
their heartbreak
    in my own

can you not feel
mercy for their
    wretched lives

for what if the real
monsters are those
    that point fingers

and sharp arrows
at those who look
    peculiar

what if the *mitos*
are merely monsters

KERANÁ

    of our own making

what if the true
monsters live
    within us all

what does
that make
    us

ñandejára

what does
    that make

me

POKÕI

Seven brothers
seven deadly
    sins

    cursed with
    scales, fang
        and fear

but perhaps
fear is only
    the façade

    how does one
    look past
        dreadful gaze

to see the
terror in
    their eyes

    how does one
    look beyond
        the horror

KERANÁ

to see the
broken
        heart within

        for what is
        sin but fear
                of failure

and
what are
        monsters

        but men
                made

wrong

CHAPTER 2
Teju Jagua

Lord of Caverns and Fruits

TEJU JAGUA

I cannot
help but
    wonder
what
freedom
    tastes
like

as I sit
alone
    with
darkness
bearing
down on me

do they not
wonder why I
    sit atop
this mound
of gold

why I hoard
    this shiny
treasure

TEJU JAGUA

which mankind
claims brings
fulfillment

I roll in
mounds of
it, absorbing
its shine but
      not its joy

this heavy
      body
my eternal
shackle

these
      fiery eyes
my curse

these
infernal
      heads my
my bane

for when I
lift one
up in

        greeting
they scream
        and run
from me

and   yet my
incandescent
gaze
        is just
a reflection
of my
desire
to see and
        be seen
I do not
wish to kill

but just to
catch a glimpse
of their face
        to taste
their *alegría*
        to know
their *tristeza*

I am not a
        monster

but this
twisted form
says otherwise

what then
is there for me
but to languish
       in my pain

alone
       solito
alone

FRUIT AND HONEY

There is
the essence
      of springtime
in *la miel*

if you close
your eyes
you can taste
      the colors
and the
dancing
feet of
      bees

there is
the essence
      of summer
in vine
ripe fruit

if you breathe
in the fragrant
olor you can
      almost see

TEJU JAGUA

the plant
on which
      it grows

there is
an empty
promise
      of sunshine
and fulfillment

in that
      which you
cannot

      have

LIZARD BRAIN

Breathe in
        darkness
breathe out
        despair

        one brain
to torment me
would be plenty
but there are seven

seven   heads
seven   minds
seven   reasons
        to overthink

so I retreat
back into
        the chasm
that lies
within
        my chest
where a heart
is meant to be

instead
a cavern
steeped in
      silence

until the
thoughts
come
crawling in
      uninvited
once again

they say
that ancient
      trauma
is stored

within
the   deepest
parts of
the   mind

lizard brain
they   call it
and I know
what
they   mean

SEVEN LEGENDARY MONSTERS

my heads
stand guard
over   every
        thought

anxiety
      arousal
alert

one too tired
to   lift
one too wired
to   sleep

all of them
on edge
      vigilant
driving me
      insane

how does
      mankind
live with this

without trying
to   bite
their

>   own
> heads off

> how do I go
> on   living
> with this
> deformity

> both within
>   and without

> breathe in
>   darkness

> breathe out
>   despair

ON CURSES

I think
I   would
prefer to
be a
      monster

than cursed
to be   mild
and   meek

but still I
must   live
with this
      monstrous
form

what I
wouldn't
give   to
be a
      mindless
beast
killing and
      ravaging

TEJU JAGUA

with
        impunity

instead
I sit in *la*
oscuridad

        shadows
bearing down
and ponder
        my mortality

cursed with
        consciousness
wrought with
        weakness

a curse
        within
a curse

CAÑA Y MIEL

Intoxication
calls my
        name

the   abyss
beckons with
honeyed
        fingers

nectar of
the immortals
        dripping
from my
        lips

sickly sweet
and   potent
I cannot resist
        this ichor

from fount
on forest floor
my   vice
springs eternal

TEJU JAGUA

caña y miel

my   lumbering
form dragging
as I make   my
way through
     darkness

to drink the
sacred sap
that courses
through
     my veins

you would not
     understand
the way I devour
it, the way it
     devours me

how can
I be judged
for what
I do   when

mortals
hand me

the   key
to their own
cages
        willingly

an offering
to placate me
only   serves
to inflame
my   hunger

my lust
      for more

che vare'a
      I am hungry

ja'umina
      let's eat

BURIED TREASURE

There are
        parts of me
I've locked
away

deep
underground
like buried
        treasure

the parts
of me that
once were
shiny and
        new

now lie
tarnished
        tired
sore

crushed like
my dreams

SEVEN LEGENDARY MONSTERS

      when I
was small

puppy
      heads
drooping
drooling
      on my
mother's
      lap

until I was
too big
to hold
      too sharp
too wild

how far can
a mother's
love   extend

for her
      most
monstrous
child

TEJU JAGUA

how long
can she
pretend
    to care

when
disgust
    sours her
maternal
    care

I see her
eyes
    averted
hiding her

abhorrence
of my big
    toothy
grin

why won't
she meet
    my eyes

can't she
see *mis*

SEVEN LEGENDARY MONSTERS

lágrimas

falling
as shiny
      golden
shards

the vestiges
of treasure
in my
      pain

can't she
hear the echo
      of sorrow
in my howl

the music
of   madness
in my
      mind

my soul
hidden deep
      beneath
this twisted
form

TEJU JAGUA

deep
        underground

like buried
        treasure

CAVE OF THE HEART

      They say
that your
eyes   can get
accustomed
to the night

but not
      in total
darkness

within this
      cavern
this eternal
echoing
      void

the gloom
is   slowly
driving me
      insane
it's
blinding me

for I have

TEJU JAGUA

not two
eyes but
      many

all straining
to catch
the faintest
      glimpse

a crack
      a crevice
a glint

searching for
      something
that isn't
      there

for nothing
ever pierces
      the depth
of shadow that
surrounds me

no one
      ever hears
it when

SEVEN LEGENDARY MONSTERS

    I scream

in the darkness
no one
ever comes

as despair
evolves into
       utter fear

for they are
too afraid
of myths
       of me

to dare
       to try
to save
a life

deep in
the cave
       of my
heart

TEJU JAGUA

darkness
        reigns

it makes
        me
truly
        monstrous

CHAPTER 3
Mbói Tu'ĩ

Lord of Waterways
and
Aquatic creatures

MBÓI TU'Ĩ

Half of me
aching to fly
               and yet

this   heavy
scaled body
weighs me
        down

torpid and
land-borne

escamas and
       plumas a
contradiction of
nature's laws

when all I want
is   the freedom
     of the skies

away from this
wretched   *pantano*
that drags me

MBÓI TU'Ĩ

      deeper into
its depths

I wish I
weren't   so
aware of my
own
limitations

my failure to
      launch

why am I
built to yearn
for that which

I cannot
     have

SQUAWK

In the darkness
no one ever
hears   it
when I
        scream

in the wetlands
no one
        ever comes

I am cursed
to be alone
los pececitos
        pecking
at my bones

swimming
        through
the shadows
        of my mind

like the *fantasmas*
of what
might   have   been

MBÓI TU'Ĩ

horrid thoughts
swirling
       currents
pulling me

down into the
murky waters
       of despair

how do I
keep my head
above   water

how do I
stay   afloat
in rising tides

how do I
keep   on
swimming

when there is
no reason to
       go on

brilliant silver
glints of fins

and eyes   in the
gloomy water

the only light
that pierces my
      desperation

in the darkness
no one
      ever
hears it
when I
      scream

in the wetlands
no one
      ever
      comes

who saves
the monsters

from
      themselves

VARE'A

The waters
of the
        Paraná
hold an ancient
    vare'a
a hunger

deep within
their   currents
there is a longing
        to devour

along the
        river's edge
a face appears
of a   girl

so beautiful
that the tides
        themselves
are jealous of
her   reflection

they envy

her ability to
rise
        above
and swim
against
the current

how   can I
resist such
a   treasure
how   can I
deny her
        appeal

Naipi is
her   name
and I long to
embrace her
        hold her
in my coils

and   so I
will have
her
as my wife
        I will not
be denied

MBÓI TU'Ĩ

for who
        can
resist the will
of
        Mbói Tu'ĩ

who can
forbid   me
from taking
        what I
am owed

let their
fear   be my
good fortune
        let her
beauty be
my bounty

and my
        sacrifice

TARUBA

I met   my
lover along
river's
        edge

her face
reflected in
the   water
was the
        most

beautiful
thing
I had ever
        seen

what *suerte*
that she
        agreed
to be mine

        but then
from depths
of

MBÓI TU'Ĩ

darkness
rose   a beast

so horrifying
that   we were
both
    petrified
frozen in
time

as he   snatched
her in his
coils
    he looked
me in the eye

in his
    fearsome
gaze I saw an
ancient pain

the   echoes
of what happens
    to a man
left in solitude
for far
    too long

SEVEN LEGENDARY MONSTERS

the fear
of being
      alone
can drive
even a
      deity
to evil
      deeds

NAIPI

I am
        petrified
of losing myself
of dying
        without
knowing

what
life, what
        love
could be like

how could I
have known
        that my
reflection in

the waters of the
river would
be my
        downfall

that to love
would be my

SEVEN LEGENDARY MONSTERS

    fate

that to lose
would be my
        curse

that to die
would be my
        destiny

how can they
be so heartless
        as to
tear me
from the one
        I love

how can they
be so   cruel
to ones
they do not
        even know

my Taruba
this monster
would

MBÓI TU'Ĩ

    kill him, but

don't they know
death is
    preferable

to having
lived without
    love

let them try
to keep us
    apart

they will
learn the
    hard way

even *un*
rio holds a
    secret

even *una*
piedra has a
    heart

SEVEN LEGENDARY MONSTERS

that cannot be
      broken

rohayhu

IGUAZÚ

From gaping
maw of
    y guazú

big water
a rainbow
    springs

the last
defiance of
my failed
    love

how can she
a mere mortal
have defied
    a deity

what does
this foolish
boy have to
offer that I
    cannot

SEVEN LEGENDARY MONSTERS

from first
glimpse I felt
still water
      move

my serpentine
form
undulating
      with pleasure

to see her
glowing face
reflected in
      my depths

cause me to
rise up, defying
all the promises
I made to my
      aquatic kin

and carve out
a new world of
possibility
      all for her

MBÓI TU'Ĩ

I must have
gone mad
to split *la tierra*
      itself

to gorge myself
on muddy
banks and jagged
      rocks

to plunge
headfirst
into the earth's
gaping
      garganta

my course
forever altered
falling, failing
      downwards

into the abyss of

      Iguazú

ARKO IRIS

Doomed
to remain
      ethereal

I lift my head
      to receive
the sun's kiss

it burns
like the touch
      of your lips
now frozen in
petrified stone

droplets   change
states and become
air, like the
whisper
of   your name
on the wind

a deliquescence
      of love
the purest form

MBÓI TU'Ĩ

of   adoration

my kaleidoscope
heart is wrapped
up in condensation
      and shards of
prismatic light

I give to you
my soul to
      bridge the
gap between
two worlds

stretching out
      a hand to the
heavens I await
my other half

to join with me
in an ecstatic
      burst of color
and light

dancing and
      shimmering

SEVEN LEGENDARY MONSTERS

petei árko íris

a rainbow
　　　　appears
in the mist

CHAPTER 4
Moñái

Lord of the Open Fields

MOÑÁI

It is said
that serpents
are related to
      birds

is that why
I am hypnotized
by plume and
feather, leaf
      and tree

and the way
the   wind
sings between
the   *lapacho*
blossoms

or is it
that life has
dissolved
      mis piernas

leaving me
forever bound

MOÑÁI

to slink and
      slither

instead of
reaching to
    el cielo

these ignorant
men, these fools
they
      mock me

lord of air
they say but
here I am
      cursed

to stay
      forever
on the ground
never knowing
      freedom

they will never
      know
the longing
that I have

to

      just

           fly

                  away

ANTENNAE

They never
see me coming
pretty feathered
      jewels

antennae
poised to tempt
them from their
      nests

against
better judgment
they heed my
      call

huesitos
ensnared by
hypnotizing
      colored rays

forked tongue
whispering
lies to lure
      them in

SEVEN LEGENDARY MONSTERS

ignoring
coiled muscles
obscured by vibrant
      leaves

until they get
too close and
      SNAP

the trap is sprung

      my trick is done

¡*opáma!*

PLUMAS

They say hope
       is a thing
with *plumas*

but have you
       ever heard
it sing

or does it come
    to roost and ruffle
in early morn

does it build a nest
    within a cage
of bones and skin

to lay a clutch
       of memory
and sin

what fools
       are they to
set their

SEVEN LEGENDARY MONSTERS

hopes
       on such a
fragile thing

for feathers
       are light as
yvytú,

       but
gravity
       still binds
them to this earth

the urge
       to reconnect
with solid ground

hidden within
       hollow quills
and trembling bones

tethered
       to this land
like naval string

where they lie
       victim to the

MOÑÁI

snares of fate

lying in wait in
        shadows of
limb and bough

where feathered
        serpent lies
in wait

to unhinge jaw and
        swallow your
dreams whole

not in pieces
        but in peace
you now shall lie

within this field
        with naught
but *flores*

to mark your
        unlucky
grave

PRANKSTER

Weak minds
can so
easily be
      led astray

fighting over
petty things
and senseless
      squabbles

like *buitres*
picking at
each other's
      bones

why did they
make me
lord over such
      payasos

any child
could spring
this trap with
      cunning words

MOÑÁI

of envy and
deceit, lies
        and jealousy

I take their
tesoros
       with a smile

while they
point fingers
in the wrong
       direction

ma'ena
how simple
       how cruel
these pranks
       I play

RIBCAGE

      The deadliest
trap is hidden
within
      the mind

      with a whisper
of self-doubt
the bars start
      closing in

      the walls
crumble and
floor beneath
      you shifts

      and everything
you've sought
to build comes
      crashing down

      how fragile
this structure
how helpless
      this heart

MOÑÁI

    a cage of ribs
only protects
from deadly
    blows

    doubt and fear
still find the
cracks between
    your bones

    the perfect
trap is the
one you
    already know

HORNED SERPENT

      The devil
you know
is better

      than the
devil you
don't

      but what
about the
devil

      you
think you
know

      but who
turns out
to be a

      trickster
lord in
disguise

MOÑÁI

      what devilry
is this

nde rasóre!

LOOT

What is
love but not
      mere loot

to hoard
within the cave
      of heart

and proudly
flaunt on
hands like
      jewels

being denied
this treasure
makes
      men rage

against one
another in
      fits of envy

wars have waged and
      cities burned

MOÑÁI

over this
incalculable
       treasure

why not
add one
       more

*¿por qué
       no?*

CHAPTER 5
Jasy Jateré

Lord of the Siesta

JASY JATERÉ

Ñembosarái
    che ra'a
come play
with me

my friend
I am here
    waiting
for you

beneath
shady
mango tree

no one
    will know
that I
snuck you
from your bed

the *siesta* is
    thick upon
them like
honey

JASY JATERÉ

weighing
        down
their eyes
in sleepy
trance

but you
        you are
not asleep
can you
hear me
whistle

beware the
        Jasy Jateré
they say
but I am
        nothing
more than
a boy

come
        we can
jump and
skip and
        sing

and feast
>   on golden
candied
treats

away from
>   rule of belt
and *chancla*
reign

where
>   naughty
children
>   never get
to play

come play
>   with me
che ra'a

I am
>   waiting

ñembosarái

THE CHILD

Beneath
        blue-eyed
innocence

and radiant
        crown of
golden hair

lurks a
        soul steeped
in unholy deeds

his child-like
        guise betrays
perfidy and guile

beware the
        tapping on
window pane

for the face you
        see is not one
of pure intent

what *sombras* pass
        behind those
plaintive eyes

what pain
        lies beneath
that mild gaze

waiting for
        you to turn
him away

a spurned
        child can
wreak havoc

for the fear of
        exclusion
can cause

the most
        gentle soul
to turn

to evil
        deeds

JASY'S SONG

Jasy why
are your
eyes so
       blue

they hold
the key to
eternal
       youth

but why
oh why do
they hold
       the key

my whole
existence
owed to
       thee

so look
into my
eyes
       my dear

SEVEN LEGENDARY MONSTERS

as I
absorb
what you
      hold dear

how sweet
of you
to come
      and play

with the
Jasy
      Jateré

SIESTA

      Sleep my
child or
you   shall
be tempted

Jasy Jateré
      will come
to entice
you   from
your dreams

secret you
away
      to play
the game

that starts
in fun   and
      ends in fear

the game
that   only
naughty
children play

SEVEN LEGENDARY MONSTERS

        beware
my child
the evil
that   lurks

beneath
        the cover
of the *siesta*
hour

as sleep
claims
you, be wary of
he who
        lurks
within dreams

hidden under
cover of
        heat and
rustling
leaves

Jasy
        whistles

MITA'I

Youth is
      wasted
on the young

I am
an old soul
trapped
      for
all eternity
within
      this
child's body

my heart
      grows
weary of
the   game
my bones
      creaking
feel the
      phantom
ache

of longing

SEVEN LEGENDARY MONSTERS

for   repose
but I am
      doomed
to never
      sleep

until I
      find
a companion
to   help
me pass my
      days

the shadows
      lengthen
sun reclines
insects
      trill
a shrieking
      lullaby

as the
      siesta
presses down
      humid
fingers on
tired
      eyes

JASY JATERÉ

enter Jasy
seeking only
just to
        play
among mankind
but they
        know
my name

and therefore
        never let
their children
run away
        with me

is it my fate
to be forever
        alone
forever
        shunned
from society by
my   birth
this
        curse

but the
        children
are too
curious to
know   fear
too innocent
to
        avoid
my trap

a whistle
        and
a tap upon
a window
pane

and they
        come
to me
all
        too
willingly

SILBATO

An *urraca*
        sings in
silence
the jungle
        listens

it mimics
the sound of
        savagery
beneath
the fronds
of forest
        glade

laughter cut
        short
by screams
a thin wail
and helpless
        sobs

the sound
of a lonely
        soul

SEVEN LEGENDARY MONSTERS

driven to
evil
      deeds

the sound
of
      someone
with nothing
left to
      lose

SOLITUDE

Why does
no one want
      to play
with me

here in the
      depths of
forest green

to sing and
dance, leap
      and fall

I do not
mean to
      cause them
harm but
      soledad

sparks my
curiosity and
my   heart
leads me
      astray

SEVEN LEGENDARY MONSTERS

what would
happen if I
      were to
take them
off the well-
tread   path

into darkness
where brother
evil lies
      in wait

it's not my
fault they
      are so fragile

or if they
cannot outrun
      evil beasts
deep within
      the forest glade

it is no
fault of mine

      play with me

CHAPTER 6
Kurupí

Lord of Fertility and Sexuality

KURUPÍ

Led by
        one head
or the other
pleasure always
on my   mind

it's not my
        fault I was
built this way
my cursed   body

endowed with
        what men
could only
wish for in
their   dreams

so why do
        women look
at me like
I'm a   freak

why do they
        laugh and

KURUPÍ

make fun   of
my monstrous
form

they don't dare
      do that to
mis hermanos
the real
monsters

and so I take my
      justice out
on their
supple   forms
as they lie
      sleeping

I plant my
      seed within
claim their
      sacred mounds
and mouths and
rounded   bellies

to incubate   my
      monstruos

and cause them
to   curse and
question

lay the blame
        on false and
unfaithful men

now they do
        not laugh
but weep

at my
        power
and my
            curse

PYHARE

Is pleasure
        not a
right

is passion
        not a
purpose

I am held
to blame
        but it
was you
who sought
me   out

telling
        lies to
mask   your
shame
        your
sinful nature

SEVEN LEGENDARY MONSTERS

for when
darkness
      falls
your truth
      awakens

window
      cracked
waiting for
a   lover's
forbidden
      touch

lying prone
on *sábanas*
a   sheen of
sudor
      upon
your brow
      furrowed
with intent

      hands
exploring
darker places

KURUPÍ

slick   and
         insatiable

hands that
delicately
       sculpt
sweetness
from sullen
       flesh

kneading
like bread
       baked
in the heat
of   desire

       braided
and rising
ready
       to be
devoured

who is to
say   what
wickedness
you might
       invite

into your
>> bed
this night

ko pyhare

no one will
ever   know
who came
>> to call
within
the   cover
of darkness

when the
>> heart of
night falls
open like
>> your
thighs

who is to
say   what
monstrosity
this   crime
of passion
>> might

KURUPÍ

endow

is this not
the   most
delicious
      sin

come
      my love

let me in

SACRED SERPENT

Pleasure snakes
its way up
        spine

like sacred
serpent
        lost

within the
jungles of your
        thighs

where dark
thoughts
        bloom
and honey
        drips

        blushing
petals
        opening
with   an
eagerness
        to share

KURUPÍ

seed and
stamen

waiting for
      the tongue
of bird or
      bat to
plunder

sweet release
      deep inside
moist
caverns

      where
dedicated
endeavor brings
      about

the constriction
of serpentine
muscles
deep
      within

to come to
climax with a

SEVEN LEGENDARY MONSTERS

    gasp

within the
hallowed circle of
    your shrine

the spirit
rises and is
    reborn

and yet
    some
claim it is
    impure

to seek this
most holy
    union

but *maldad* is only
in the
mind of
    man

for sacred are
the ways of the
    serpent

KURUPÍ

not just a curse
but a promise

of nature's

        fertile
inheritance

DIVINING ROD

Your form
seeks me out
        like a divining rod
        probing for
that secret fount
        deep within

dripping
        with dew
        the eternal spring
of *pasión*
escondida
        transforms

my love into
        adoration

        sublimation
enacted by
        your will
        returns to
ground as
        gentle rain

KURUPÍ

I feel the
        effervescence
as it rises
        in dewy

spheres

        pressed
between
        mis labios
I pull
        deeply

bringing
the water
        of life
to surface

to explode
        on thirsty
tongue

sacred *fuente*
        gushing
like the source
        of life itself
in *mi boca*

SEVEN LEGENDARY MONSTERS

       for I am earth
but I am
       also yours
       and you are
going to
       turn me

into
       water

TATAKUA

Fire deep
      within
ignites

the embers of
      my heart
ablaze with
lust   I rise

why do
you insist on
stoking the
      inferno

risking the
burn   of
reckless
desire

why do
you tempt
me   so

and spark
the maelstrom

of   my lust

a firestorm
        blazing
at my core

as though
the air
itself is
        consumed

by hungry
tongues
       of flame

within the
       tatakua
of my soul

that fiery
furnace deep
       within

I burn
       for
            you

VESSEL

Women
are   told
from the
      moment
of our birth

that we are
nothing
      more
than sculpted
vessels

fired clay
      cerámica
iron   red and
ash   black and
chalky white
      wrapped
in cotton
      and lace

our beauty
proven in our
      purity

SEVEN LEGENDARY MONSTERS

our fragility
proven in our
      fall

and what
happens
      when
we break
shatter
fall to
      pieces
in the hardness
of your
      hands

is this broken
vessel
      that
once held
value
no longer
      worthy
of exhibition

I see you
trying to
put the

KURUPÍ

    pieces
back together
only for
them
to crumble
    into
splintered bone
and sharp
    edges

they call it
    a shame
as if the
    verguenza
was yours
alone
    to bear

they call it
    a loss
as if it was
your   fault
that
    he could
not handle you
with
    care

they call it
        a theft
as if you were
something to
be   stolen
something to be
claimed

as if he
        could
hide the
pieces
        of your
worth in
his pocket
        and
call it his
        prize

but hear me:

nothing you
hold
        within
the *ánfora*
of your chest

KURUPÍ

can ever
        be stolen
from you

your body
is no
        bounty
to be claimed
no
        plunder
to be taken

and I know
it's hard to
feel
        whole
when your
life is
        reduced
to *pedazos*
on the
        ground

but I will
        not
see you

crumble into
        dust

daughter of
        the earth
and sky

you were
        made of
ash and clay

never
        forget

who
        you are

KUÑA MBARETÉ

Why are
women always
    held to blame
for mankind's
    sins

inciting
violence to
our flesh
    the urge
to rip and tear
and
    claim

like some
sacred right
    is taken
from us
by our birth

and given
to   men as
if mere loot
not   soul

SEVEN LEGENDARY MONSTERS

itself

our dignity
torn   asunder
under iron
       rule of
fist and fear

this monster
       Kurupi
he laid me
       bare
and broke me

used me for
his evil deed
       and left
me raw
and   ruined

am I then
       condemned
for   actions
taken   not
my own

the blame

KURUPÍ

laid squarely
at my feet

for   stirring
his passion
for   merely
        existing

when monsters
lurk among
        mortals

hiding fang
and claw behind
        dark eyes
and empty
        promises

how then
        is it my
fault
what I wore
or what I
said or if I
        looked
        too enticing

it is not my
job to make
myself
       less
       to avoid
              my own
destruction

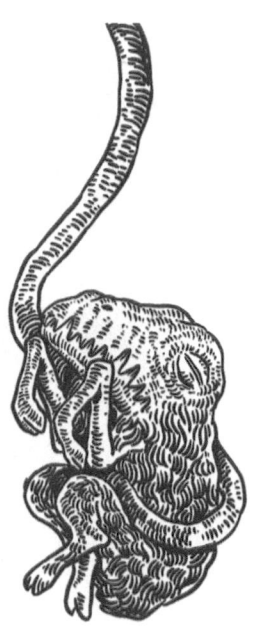

CHAPTER 7
Ao Ao

Lord of Hills and Mountains

AO AO

Why are
the children
of the earth

       always held
to blame for
mankind's
       sins

my task, since
before my
fangs   fully
formed was
given to me by
       che sy
my mother

she said
wild one, protect
this earth, these
       forests
glades and

AO AO

fertile *cerros*

from those
who would
seek to
      cut them
down and
      destroy
them

guardian of
the hills and
las montañas
      you shall
be and I am
      that

a sacred oath
whose words
I henceforth
      shall abide

though it may
cast me as evil

SEVEN LEGENDARY MONSTERS

      in the eyes
of humankind

so my teeth and
claw and hoof
and fang are put
      to use
in the pursuit
of evil men

those who
      ravage
rout and kill
these forests
with
      impunity

mindless of
their hedonistic
      destruction
of Tupã's creation

and they say
I am the
      monstruo

I am just

AO AO

      protecting
what is mine

you fools

can you
      hear
the cry of
vengeance
echo through
the wild
      green
hills

ao ao

it is the
cry of one
with nowhere
left
      to
           run

it is the
sound a heart
makes

before
>	it
>		breaks

UNTAMED

There is
hunger in the
      hunt

there is
passion in
      pursuit

there is
victory in
      venganza

an absolution
      of sorts

in the
knowledge
      that you are

what they say
      you are

authenticity
in every grunt

    and howl

monstrous
deadly
    wild

the essence of
nature in fang
    and fear

you bow
to no
    master

but the
earth
    itself

you kneel
to no
    throne

but the
sky
    above

AO AO

you are

indomable

KA'AGUY

The forest
screams
        there
is no one
left
to   hear

no   witness
to this
        grief
eons in
        the
making

the   ax
lets out
a   mighty
grunt
as it
        cuts
the   air
itself
and lands
its fatal

AO AO

       blow

the sound
an   omen
a rhythmic
       drumbeat
of barbaric
souls

too   far
from grace
to   know
what they
have
       done

for this
the
       earth
will exact
a
       price

a life for
       a life

a sentence

SEVEN LEGENDARY MONSTERS

carried
out

by   one
they call
a   beast

and yet
      and yet

if I am
      beast

then what
are
      they

PINDOVY

In the midst of
amaranthine
      darkness

Tupã stretched
out his hand
      and life
sprang forth

in the form of
pindovy
      primordial
palms

five pillars
      of creation
standing tall
bursting forth
from bosom
      of the earth

two to
serve as mighty
      thrones

of heaven

one each in
the North
        and South
and one
in the
        Center

el corazón
of the world
        whose roots
embedded
and intertwined

formed the
foundations of
        the universe

and whose
        branches
outstretched
and expansive

cradle
the sky
        above

HEARTS OF PALM

The palm tree
holds in
loving arms
       a heart
encased
in husks of
steel

fibers thick
surrounding it
       to cushion
from the
hardest blow

oh, that
mi corazón
could be so
       sturdy

when
the winds of
change blow in
       and clouds
obscure

SEVEN LEGENDARY MONSTERS

the sun

and when
        night
billows in
in dusky
        cloaks

that it might still
        hold hope
within
like the hearts
of palm
        that will
never run
dry

AO

    At birth
we emerge
from womb
naked and
without sin

    as children
we play
unclothed and
unashamed

do you
remember
    the moment
that you become
aware of your
own mortality

    when you
rushed to hide
your true self

SEVEN LEGENDARY MONSTERS

to put on
    ao - ropa
clothing

to hide
your nakedness
to conceal
your inner
    spark

    has it ever
occurred to you
the monster
they call the
Ao Ao

    the one who
is said to
steal clothes
from lines
thinking them
    human

might merely
    be our own
unconscious
mind

AO AO

    seeking
to hide the
shame of what
we once were

    and what
we are now
afraid
    to be

YVYTY

Shadows
        lurk in
the hands
of these hills

the dark
        places
in between
the verdant
green of
leaf and
        limb

and the
        crevices
formed by
the tongue
of time

these hills
        hold secrets
like sealed
        sepulcros
no one knows

AO AO

what they
        might find

lurking just
        beyond
the next
        bend
behind
the farthest
        hill
within
the deepest
        cavern

no one knows
        when they
might hear

the sound
of hooves
        pounding
in your ears

as monsters
        ride in

CHAPTER 8
Luisón

Lord of Death and Dying

LUISÓN

Fear is
a double
      edged sword
it can drive
men to honor
      or to hate

to flee or
      to fight
and they are
always
hunting
      me

there is
      nowhere
to run from
las esquinas
      of my mind
the ones that
      twist me

into lurid
shapes, plant

LUISÓN

daggers where
teeth should
      be, make hair
sprout from
the face I
      long to
hide

so I stalk
cemeteries
      tombstoned
shadows
hiding my
      hideousness

destined
      to hold the
shape
of death
      in the minds
of man

siete hijos
      seven sins
seven ways
      to learn to hate

SEVEN LEGENDARY MONSTERS

who am I
the wolf
        or the man
the terror or
        the reckoning

do I give
up or give in
        to my beastly
urge to become
        the nightmare

how could I ever
        be more evil than
the monster they
        imagine me
to be

WEREWOLF

I'm a *monstruo*
I know you
      don't believe it
but I should
      come with
warning signs
and locked
doors
      and padded
      walls

aléjate
you don't know
      the danger
that flows
wickedly
      through
my   veins

inside of me
there is a latent
      sickness
that consumes
      my entire

being

it transforms
        me into
the   wild
creature
lurking in the
corners
        of my
imagination

an addict is
always
an addict
        and sober
        is just another
        word for thirsty

my mind is
too thirsty
        to admit
        I am capable
my heart is
too thirsty
        to allow
        me to love

LUISÓN

why should I trust
in these
parched hands
that have proven
      treacherous

and in this
      deadly heart
that has damaged
more than
      one hapless
      victim

sometimes I cry
before
      I fall asleep
and wake up
      to the phrase
I'm better than this!
      carved on the
surface of
my   skin

this disease still
consumes me
      every day
the   craving

increases
the temptation
       in my cellular
       tissue

       but I have
       to live
I have
to survive
       to do less
would be
an act of
cowardice

sometimes
       living
means purging
       the toxins
to make
space for
       the light to
       shine   in

and sometimes
       living is
not doing what
you want

      when you know
that the only
      person
you're hurting is
yourself

I don't want
attention
      or your pity
and
I don't need
      to justify
my story

I'm a *monstruo*
      I'm fighting
to retain my
mortality

seeing the blood
      proves it

I'm still alive
still human
      still able to feel

LUNAR ECLIPSE

Under blood red skies
dragging specters
one   by   one
out of the depths

of mind crypts
the   vaults
haunted with
grief and guilt

screams of
past   and   future
echo in
the dark well
of my mind

tormented souls
dragging
      chains of
regret   and   fear
bonds of guilt
laced with poison

LUISÓN

shadow work
eclipses hope
as *la luna*
goes   behind
       the earth's
mantle of
darkness

light   and   dark
at war for a brief
moment in time

this too
      shall pass

SEVENTH SON

How does
one break
      a cycle of
myth and
      legend

how do
I atone
      for sins
not my own

why must
this beastly face
      still cause
people to
      flinch away

Luisón
seventh son
      they whisper

their eyes
flicking from mine to
      hands and ears

LUISÓN

as if to see
fur sprouting

as if to see
claws emerge
from these
        wretched
hands

but I am just
a man no
        more no less
destined to
live in a land
        where *monstruos*

are more
        sacred than
the sins committed
by evil
        men

what can I
        do to
prove my
        pain

SEVEN LEGENDARY MONSTERS

what can I
      say to
show my
humanity

it's enough to
      make
me howl

SHAPESHIFTER

    My bones
are shifting in
    my skin

    this bed can't
hold me
    anymore

    having outgrown
these lies
    I tell myself

    like the moon
sheds her skin
    each month

    and emerges
large and
    ravenous

    consuming
shadow
    in her greed

SEVEN LEGENDARY MONSTERS

        to claim
the night as
        her own

        if she
can face
        her fears

        and shine
so then
        can I

CEMENTERIO

Wandering
through rows of
crumbling stone

my thoughts
buried deep
as the bones
beneath   my
    feet

I hear the
echoes of
the   past in
     the way the
wind whistles
through the
     tombstones

perhaps
     the monster
that lurks here
is not who
     they say

not one born

of fur   and fang
          but rather
born of
grief
          that lurks
always in
the back of
          my mind

the most
terrifying
          specter of
them all
          is the one
you cannot
          see

ON DEATH

What is death
but the physical
manifestation
      of change

the end of
a cycle that
is destined
      to repeat

like the
phases of
the moon
      itself

then why do
men fear it
as if looking
      mortality

in the eye is
akin to lighting
themselves
      on fire

and watching
sparks rise
and ashes
       fly away

how can you
fight your
inevitable
       fate

is it fear
that makes
your bones
       tremble

or dread
of what
legacy you
       leave behind

know this:

the final
word is the
one that is
       remembered

LUISÓN

and so
I am here
to grant you
        immortality

for even the
worst man is
granted kindness
        in death

let me
                in

CHAPTER 9
Porãsy

Sublime Sacrifice

PORÃSY

No one
        ever asks
to be a martyr

no one ever
        wants to die

so what
        do you do
when the heavens
demand it
        of you
I will rise
to the occasion

give my
        body over
to the darkness
if you demand
        it of me

but no one
        ever asks to
be a hero

PORĀSY

so what does
that mean for
    all the men
and women

    the ones in
the stories they
tell around the
    fireside in
song and dance

    when there is
no other choice
but the one that
    is impossible
to make

that doesn't
imply free will

    only a trap
of time
place and
    consequence

no one ever
        goes to battle
thinking: will they
remember me

no one
is pondering
        their legacy
while they are
bleeding out

no one
is a hero
in their
        final
throes

        what do
los héroes
think about

as they
        feel the
fatal wound

PORÃSY

Ñande Sy
       Sypavé

mother
be here with
      me now

hold my
hand as
      I lie
dying

TUMÉ ARANDÚ

Is wisdom
just another word
for sacrificing
all that you
      love

for what is wisdom
if not the
implication
      of pain

for who is a wise man
but the one who
has to make
the hardest
      choice

I did not
ask for this
weight to be
placed on my
      heart

PORĀSY

sabio, mago
they call me
wise one
savior of
        our people

so why am I
the one who
has to make
        the call

why am I
the one who
has to die a
        million deaths

knowing that
my actions
shape
        the world

why am I
the only one
        that sees

that the wisest
course
>of action

is the one
that hurts
>the most

JAHARI GUA'A

Under Tupã's
      watchful eye
I hold my breath
and flutter through
the forest canopy

preparing
to bring words of
wisdom on
      wing and
feather

divine
messenger
am I   the
guacamayo

for no one
else can hide
      in plain sight
with such colorful
plumage

but in jewel
>	hued forest
I sit and watch
unseen among
the frothy greens

of *hojas* and scarlet
>	*flores* face me
upturned, patiently
awaiting my signal

to let out a
>	mighty
squawk

the piercing
cry a warning
and sacred
>	promise

that only
Porãsy can rid
>	the
world of
such   evil

that she must
die to   set
        us free

who would
have guessed

that a mere bird
would bear this
        burden

for I am but the
        mouthpiece
of the heavens

jahari gua'a

KA'A RUVICHA

Do you still
know the
    ancient ways
of root
    and branch
and flower

cast your
gaze   downward
and behold, I am
the ruler of
    them all

I will grant
you   courage
in both life
    and death

for the power
held   in my
    leaves is
enough to *matar*
    or *curar*

or to send
>	you into
spiral dance

small wonder
>	then, that I
am held holy
still   revered

>	among the ones
whose feet still
walk the   wild
>	path of sacred
knowledge

those who
still sing
>	*alabanzas*
to the earth

shaman
>	*cacique*
the keepers of
ancient wisdom

know my power
>	held not in

el cielo but
here on
      the ground

      ka'a
plant
      ruvicha
king

for I   alone
shall grant you
      courage
in your final
      throes

eat me
      and
you shall know
my *magia*

imparted to
      you
long ago by
      Tupã

PORĀSY

you hold my
>	worship in
the palm
of your
>	hand

and you hold
>	my secrets
within
blood
>	and bone

TEMIKUAVE'E

Step one
        deception

        step two
                sacrifice

step one
        one foot in
front of another

        step two
                try not to
        run away

step one
        I stand
before him
        Moñaí

        step two
                try not to
        show any fear

step one
> how did

I get here

> step two
> > what did I

> do to deserve
> > this fate

step one
> how do I

fool him

> step two
> > make him

> think I am
> > madly in love

step one
> here he

comes now

> step two
> > I am your

> sacrifice
> > *temikuave'e*

step one
    the taste of
blood in my
mouth

        step two
            smiling
        through lips
        that are shaking

step one
    ka'a ruvicha
grant me
courage

        step two
            I offer up
        my body to
        the divine

step one
    deception

    step

        step two
            sacrifice

       step   step

step three
ñandejara

       what is

step

       three

ÑEMENDÁPE

Seven days to
      seek
and search

seven days
to gather
all my brothers
      to heed my
call, and they come

knowing that I
the   Moñaí
can save us all

all as eager
as I to put an
end to this conflict
once and
      for all

why do I
still hesitate
before my
      fate

PORĀSY

does she know that
she must be the
      one to bridge
the divide

to offer
      herself up
as a flag of truce
as sublime
      sacrifice

who knows, but
all I want is to
      put an end to
these ceaseless
battles between
man   and *monstruo*

flesh and fang
shall no longer
      divide us with
this tryst

to end the
war one must
know thy
      enemy

and I plan
to know her
        intimately

let us begin
        with I do

KO'ÊTĨ

When I was
a child, I often
wondered
where the rivers
       drain

fearless
even then, always
wandering into
       forest grove

heedless of
the warnings
of what evil
might lurk
       within
it never crossed
       my mind

but now, that I
have nothing left
       to lose, as I
sit here in
this leafy cage

SEVEN LEGENDARY MONSTERS

to await my
destiny in
      the dawn
I let my fear
run away with the
      southern wind

crisp and cold
the air stings
      my nose
withered leaves
crackle beneath
      my feet

exquisite
corpses of
their former
      selves

I can feel
my heartbeat
in my palms

my heart pumps
contaminated
      blood
through

the rivers of
       my soul

as my lungs
gasp for breath
saving my   spirit
      from the
toxic waste of
      my   mind

the muddy rivers
drain from
      mis ojos as
tears, salty like
      river delta

wild as
jungle roots and
cold as
sky   vault

the heavens
above me
      aflame
      with sparks
the light of dawn

SEVEN LEGENDARY MONSTERS

ko'ẽtĩ
dances a
    cachaca
    behind
my eyelids
it is time to give
    my bones
unto the heavens

drowning in
    sensation
I wrap myself in
the tears of a cloud

and give myself
over to fear

as I sit
beneath
this *pindovy*

    and
await my
doom

PY'AGUASÚ

Ceremony
      done
I sit, surrounded
by evil

monstrous
forms, drunk
on   *chicha*
pliant and
      unarmed

     this is
the part where
my   courage
fails me

    coraje
that I never
    knew I
possessed
until   today

the time
has come

SEVEN LEGENDARY MONSTERS

        to
set the plan
in   motion

sneak away
and let my
        tribe
do the rest

and yet
I sit here
        with
miedo on my
        mind

it cannot
be this easy
        can it

I know deep
        down that
I am doomed
to fail

ka'a ruvicha
no   longer
in my system

PORĂSY

I must
      rely
on my own
strength
      now

py'aguasú
courage don't
      fail me

just one
more task
      and
then I can
rest

if I must
die, let it
be standing

not sitting
      here
in the darkness
surrounded
by
      monsters

SEVEN LEGENDARY MONSTERS

it all began
with I do

now let
       it end
with
       me

       it is time

MBYJA KO'Ê

They say it is
always darkest
before the dawn
      and I know
the truth
of that
      all too
            well

but what
they do
      not say
is how the
dawn feels
to be the one
      destined

to shine
      the light
into the
      darkness

so tell me
then, *Arasy*

    sky mother

why are women
        always the ones
to bear the burden
        of mankind's ills

to illuminate the
        darkness for
the ones who
        cannot see
to shine until we
we burn ourselves
        out

for those
        who do not
have the courage
to contain
        our light

sublime
sacrifice
        indeed

PORĀSY

our lives
        are but
a twinkle
in the
        heavens

and yet
        we are
the ones
        that persist

the ones
        that guide
the way
through the
        darkness

into

        the

                dawn

EPILOGUE

On Monsters and Men

When I began this epic poetry retelling of the Seven Legendary Monsters, I have to admit that I had little to go off of besides the lingering feeling deep inside me that this was a story that needed to be told. I struggled with my old friend, imposter syndrome, nearly every day. The thought of—*who am I to tell these stories?*— was very real.

So, I put it off for months, making excuses—I don't have time for this, I have another book in progress, it will be too difficult, and so on. But in the end, I decided on a whim to use it as inspiration for NaNoWriMo (National Novel Writer's Month). While it obviously fell short of the 50,000 words to win the writing competition, this story ended up clawing itself out of me in its entirety in less than a *month*. That's how badly these monsters wanted to be seen and heard.

SEVEN LEGENDARY MONSTERS

Ultimately, I decided to write this book for several reasons, the most important of which being that there are very few written retellings of Paraguayan myths. The only texts that have survived are a mixture between the original oral myths and legends and the imagination of the storytellers who have passed these stories down for generations.

The most notable, and perhaps the only true, source material, of course, being the work "Ñande *Ypy Kuéra* - Nuestros Antepasados" written over a century ago by the Paraguayan poet Narciso Ramón Colman, better known as Rosicrán.

Like Rosicrán, I have taken immense liberties with these figures. I have humanized, rather than sensationalized, these monsters in order to give a deeper meaning to the beings that roam the collective imagination of an entire country. I do this not to replace or retell the original legends, but to give them a mind of their own to tell their stories through me.

When I sat down to write this book, I intended for it to have seven chapters with seven poems each. The number seven is a predominant thread

EPILOGUE

throughout these myths, and I felt that it would be the glue that binds the story together.

As it turns out, you have before you a book with *nine* chapters total because I felt that I could not do the story justice without highlighting the incredible women who are often erased from the narrative, but who are truly as important, if not more so, than the monsters themselves.

I hope that you found some humanity within these pages, some common threads that bind us all together. For truly, *"what are monsters, but men made wrong?"*

Thank you for reading! Muchas gracias! Aguije ndéve!

COMPENDIUM OF MORTALS AND MONSTERS

THE MONSTERS

Teju Jagua: Lizard-Dog

It is said that Teju Jagua was the first son of Taú and Keraná and the oldest of the Seven Legendary Monsters of Guaraní mythology.

Because of the curse placed upon Taú by Arasy for kidnapping Keraná, Taú's descendants were forever cursed with a deformed and monstrous appearance. Thus, the pair's first son was a huge lizard with seven dog-heads and eyes that shoot out fire.

The heights and abysses of Cerro Yaguarón are his natural habitat, where he dominates his environment from the caverns carved into the limestone. According to the myths of Paraguay, he once emitted a roar so loud that the rocks on the top of the hill crumbled.

His appearance was the most horrid of all the seven brothers. However, the divine being Tupã took pity on him and tempered his ferocity by making him calm and harmless to all those outside his domain – the caverns of the local hills and mountains. His seven dog-heads and heavy body made any movement difficult, limiting his capacity to move from the caves in which he was born. Still, he was feared for his fiery gaze.

By day, he is the guardian of the surrounding forest, where it is said there was a magical spring of honey from which he feeds. He also is said to eat fruit that his brother Jasy Jateré brings him from time to time. Because of this, he is considered the lord of the caves and protector of fruit.

He is also mentioned in local legends as the protector of the precious stones and minerals found in Paraguayan soil, known as *plata yvyguy*. It is often said that his skin acquired shine by rolling in his hoard of gold and the precious stones of Itapé, ones that humankind can never seem to find as it is always buried beneath him. A valiant few go looking, but those who brave his wrath to search for his treasures are never successful.

THE MONSTERS

Mbói Tu'ĩ: Parrot-Snake

It is said that Mbói Tu'ĩ was the second son of Taú and Keraná. Born with the body of a gigantic serpent and the head of a parrot, he is known as the protector of the wetlands and aquatic creatures.

Mbói Tu'ĩ has a blood-red tongue and a vicious stare that frightens everyone who looks into his eyes. He is known by his powerful squawk which can be heard throughout the swamp, instilling terror in all who hear it.

Mboi Tui's home is the *pantanal* - the world's largest wetland system. He patrols these lands and protects the amphibious and aquatic creatures who live there.

Moñái: Feathered Serpent

It is said that Moñái was the third son of Taú and Keraná. Like his brother Mbói Tu'î, Moñái has an enormous serpent-like body but instead of a parrot's head he has two straight, colorful horns over his head, which serve as antennae and a mouth filled with needle-sharp teeth.

His dominions are the open fields. He can climb trees with ease and slide down to hunt the birds on whom he feeds and dominates with the hypnotic power of his antennas. Because of this he is often called "the lord of the air".

A prankster by nature, Moñái is considered the benefactor of thieves. He is fond of stealing and hiding the products of his misdeeds in local caves. His continuous robbing and raiding in the villages provoked great discord among the people as they all accused each other of the robberies and mysterious "disappearances" of their belongings.

Moñái also played a huge role in the conclusion of Taú and Keraná's legend. Porãsy fooled Moñái into thinking she was in love with him and agreed to marry him to save her tribe. Then, during their wedding ceremony, she tried to kill him.

It didn't work, but Keraná and Porãsy's tribe was able to lock all seven monsters attending the ceremony in the cave where it was taking place, killing them.

Sadly, this also killed Porãsy, who became a martyr to save mankind from the Seven Legendary Monsters.

Jasy Jateré: Lonely Child

It is said that Jasy Jateré was unique among his brothers in that he did not have a monstrous appearance. He is usually described as being a small man or perhaps a child, with light blonde hair and blue eyes. He is fair in appearance, sometimes described as even beautiful or enchanting, and carries with him a magical wand or staff. Like most of his brothers he dwells in the wild, and he is considered to be the protector of the yerba mate plant.

Jasy Jateré is considered to be the lord of the siesta, the traditional mid-day nap taken in many Latin American cultures. According to one widespread version of the myth, Jasy Jateré leaves the forest and wanders the villages looking for children who are not napping during their siesta. Although he is generally invisible, it is said that he shows himself to the children he finds not napping, and that any who look upon his staff fall into a trance. He also lures them into the forest with a distinctive whistle.

What happens to such entranced children differs depending upon which version of the story is told. In the fairer version of the tale, Jasy Jateré is considered a friend of such disobedient children, taking them into hidden places in the forest to play and feeding them with honey and fruit. At the end of the siesta, when all are weary from the play, Jasy Jateré gives them a magical kiss which transports them back to their beds with no memory of the experience.

Most versions of the story are less fair. Commonly, Jasy Jateré takes entranced children back to a cave where he puts out their eyes and imprisons them for an untold amount of time, sustaining them with wild fruits and berries until they become feral like animals. Still more gruesome tales say that the children are brought back to his brother Ao Ao, a cannibalistic creature who feeds upon their flesh.

These versions of the myth are told in a similar vein to the Bogeyman, designed to frighten children into being obedient and taking a nap during their siesta. Paraguayan parents are known to warn their children not to wander off alone during siesta to prevent being kidnapped by Jasy Jateré.

It is said that Jasy Jateré's power stems from the magical staff that he carries, and if one is able to take it from him, he breaks down and cries like a little child. In this state, one may ask him for the treasures that he is protecting in return for the staff, not unlike a captured leprechaun who must reward his captor with a pot of gold.

Kurupí: Virile Dwarf

It is said that Kurupí is somewhat similar in appearance to another, more popular figure from Guaraní mythology, the Pombero. Like the Pombero, Kurupí is said to be a dwarf-like creature: short, ugly, and hairy.

He makes his home in the wild forests of the region and was considered to be the lord of the forests and protector of wild animals. Kurupí's most distinctive feature, however, is a long, narrow member that is ordinarily wound several times around his waist like a belt. Due to this feature, he was at one time revered by the Guaraní as the spirit of fertility and sexuality.

Kurupí is often blamed for unexpected or unwanted pregnancies. His penis is said to be prehensile, and owing to its length he is supposed to be able to extend it through doors, windows, or other openings in a home and impregnate a sleeping woman without even having to enter the house.

This made Kurupí a scapegoat used by adulterous women to avoid the wrath of their husbands, or by single women to explain their pregnancies.

Children fathered by the Kurupí were expected to be small, ugly, and hairy much like their father, and, if male, to inherit something of their father's virility. In some cases, Kurupí is blamed with the disappearance of young women, supposedly stealing them away to his home in the forest for use in satiating his libidinous desires.

The legend of Kurupí has faded somewhat, and figures more often as part of old tales. Rarely is he blamed with impregnating women anymore, although he is sometimes used to try and frighten young girls into being chaste.

Ao Ao: Boar-Dog

It is said that the Ao Ao is a voracious boar or sheep-like creature with curly hair covering its body and a massive set of fangs. Its name is derived from the sound that it makes, howling "Ao ao ao!" when it is pursuing its victims.

The Ao Ao is considered the most deadly of the Seven Legendary Monsters, and the most bloodthirsty. Ao Ao is said to eat people as its sole source of food, feasting on human flesh and stalking people who venture into the hills alone.

The original Ao Ao is said to have profound reproductive powers. Ao Ao produced many offspring who were cursed in the same manner, and collectively they served as lords and protectors of the hills and the mountains.

It is widely believed that the Ao Ao was created to punish humans who behaved in a selfish or greedy manner by cutting down trees or plundering resources. If one encounters an Ao Ao, the beast's presence stands for divine punishment, reminding one of the importance of living in harmony with nature and other living beings.

According to most versions of the myth, the Ao Ao, upon locating a victim for its next meal, will pursue the unfortunate person over any distance or terrain, not stopping until it has had its meal. If a person attempts to escape by climbing a tree, for example, the Ao Ao will circle the tree, howling incessantly and digging at the roots until the tree falls.

In fact, according to myth, the only way to successfully escape from an Ao Ao is to seek shelter by climbing a Pindo Palm tree. This tree, also called the Queen Palm, contained some unknown power against the Ao Ao, and if its intended victim did climb one, the creature would howl in defeat and leave in search of another meal.

In some versions of the myth, the Ao Ao would feast upon disobedient children brought to it by his brother, Jasy Jateré.

The Ao Ao is also known for eating clothes off laundry lines, thinking them to be human.

Luisón: Wolf-man

It is said that Luisón was a hideous dog-like creature with razor-sharp teeth and red, glowing eyes. He feeds on cadavers he takes out of crypts and tombs in the cemetery. Luisón is rumored to have long, dirty hair that fell down to cover most of his form, pale and sickly looking skin and eyes, and accompanied by the constant, fetid odor of death and decay.

So frightening and repulsive was his appearance that his mere presence would instill terror in any unfortunate enough to encounter the beast. Even worse, after feeding on the flesh of the dead, it turns its eyes on the living, and feeds on them as well.

His name comes from the Latin word for werewolf, Lobisomem, more literally "wolf-man." What name Luisón may have had before the influence of European-based mythology is probably lost.

For those who believe in Luisón, the creature acts as a sort of Grim Reaper, whose mere presence means death will soon befall those it encounters. If Luisón passes through a person's legs, it is said, the person turns into Luisón. In some versions, Luisón only appears on Monday, Wednesday, and Friday nights.

When it is unable to find the flesh of dead animals or humans to eat, it will attack. Not only does it kill its victims, it eats their souls. This causes them to become cursed as well. Luisón was also known for feeding specifically on unbaptized children if they cannot find a meal, something that also undoubtedly evolved from the influence of Catholicism as it spread in South America.

Luisón is said to be a human until his thirteenth birthday when he gains the ability to transform into a demonic werewolf. He then lives among the townspeople as a normal human being during the day. However, on a full moon, he reverts to his beastly form, leaves his home, and begins feeding in the cemeteries, similar to the European werewolf.

THE MONSTERS

In part, the transition from the original myth to a more werewolf-like creature is because Luison was the seventh son. According to one superstition, the seventh son in a family of all boys is prone to fall victim to a curse that would turn him into a Luisón when he reaches adolescence.

Therefore, the seventh boy child is considered to be unlucky or cursed in Paraguayan society, even in modern times. Some families even killed or abandoned their seventh son for fear it would grow to have the Luisón curse, a fate considered worse than death itself.

THE MORTALS

Tupa and Arasy

The primary figure in most Guarani creation myths is Tupã, the supreme being of all creation. With the help of the divine mother Arasy, Tupã descended upon the Earth on a hill in the region of Aregúa, Paraguay. From that location he created all that is found upon the face of the earth, including the rivers, forests, and the animals.

Tupã then created humanity in an elaborate ceremony, forming clay statues of man and woman using a mixture of various plants and elements from nature, including the rich red Paraguayan soil. After breathing life into the human forms, he left them with the brother spirits of good and evil, Angatupyry and Taú, and departed.

Rupave and Sypave

The original humans created by Tupã were named Rupave and Sypave, whose names mean "Father of the people" and "Mother of the people" respectively.

The first of their sons was Tumé Arandú, considered to be the wisest of men and the great prophet of the Guaraní people. Second of their sons was Marangatú, a benevolent and generous leader of his people, and father of Keraná, the mother of the Seven Legendary Monsters.

Among the daughters of Rupave and Sypave was Porãsy, who sacrificed her own life in order to rid the world of the Seven Legendary Monsters.

Keraná and Taú

Keraná was a beautiful maiden whose name meant "sleepyhead" or "sleeping beauty." In the peaceful world of first creation, she spent her days sleeping in the rainforest, lulled to sleep by the gentle hum of the newly made birds and insects.

Her serene beauty was such that Keraná captured the attention of the spirit of evil, Taú, who fell hopelessly in love with her.

Taú decided that he must have her and set his plan into motion. To woo her, Taú transformed himself into a handsome young man and followed Keraná to where she slept in the forest. He carried with him a magic flute, which he played to entrance the young maiden. The sound of his flute awakened Keraná, who was dazzled by his beauty and by the hypnotic music he played.

Taú visited Keraná for seven consecutive days, awakening her with music and leaving her gifts in his attempt to woo her. On the seventh day, he tried to kidnap the young woman, but Angatupyry, the spirit of good, intervened to prevent it.

Angatupyry began a battle with Taú that lasted seven days in the great fields near the hills of Areguá. The fight was fierce. After six days and nights, it appeared that Angatupyry would win and good would triumph over evil.

Exhausted, Taú tried to evade the ferocious onslaughts of the spirit of good, but Angatupyry was just too strong. Taú cried out to Pytãjovái, the lord of war, to help him. Pytãjovái heeded his call and called a great bolt of lightning to descend upon the earth and strike down Angatupyry where he stood.

Taú used the distraction to escape the battle and steal Keraná away. As punishment for his crime, the celestial mother Arasy cursed him for all eternity and condemned all his offspring so that all but one of Taú's sons were born as hideous creatures.

Porãsy and Moñaí

After seven years of devastation at the hands of the Seven Legendary Monsters, Tumê Arandú saw the suffering of his people and decided to ask Tupã for help. He set off into the forest to make his plea.

Tupã heard the prayer and felt shame for what had become of his creations. He sent a message to Tumê Arandú through jahari gua'a, a macaw, that the defeat of the Seven Legendary Monsters can only be carried out by a beautiful maiden.

Tumê Arandú returned home and related what he had heard to his tribe. The youngest and most beautiful of his sisters, Porãsy, bravely volunteered to help with the plan, even if it meant sacrificing herself for the good of humanity.

To assist her in this feat, the tribe gathered the sacred plant, ka'aruvicha, and prepared an infusion from its leaves to provide strength to carry out her great deed.

When preparations were complete, Porãsy went to Moñái's cave. Moñái awoke and went out to meet her but, captivated by her beauty, did not kill her. Instead, he was so enchanted that he asked her what such a beautiful maiden like her was doing in his lair.

Porãsy, following the plan, told him that she was fascinated by the stories of his bravery that she had heard from her tribe, that she was in love with the monstrous being and that she wanted to marry him.

Moñái, dazzled by the beauty and eloquence of the young woman, agreed to marry her on the spot. Porãsy replied that she would do it on one condition: that Moñái's brothers be present at the wedding.

Moñái accepted but suggested that they marry in Teju Jagua's cave since he, due to his deformities, could not leave his dwelling. Porãsy agreed and they both set off for the grotto. The plan that Tupã had communicated to Tumê Arandú was set in motion.

For seven days Porãsy waited in the cave with Teju Jagua while Moñái searched for and gathered his other brothers. On the final night, when all the monsters were finally together, the wedding was held.

Porãsy encouraged the monsters to drink chicha, a fermented beverage made of maize (corn), and get drunk to celebrate her marriage to Moñai. Outside, in the dead of night, Tumê Arandú's warriors silently surrounded the hill where the grotto was located.

The wedding continued inside the cave under the watchful eyes of Porãsy, who pretended to drink and patiently awaited the opportunity to give the signal to her tribe. The monsters danced more and more clumsily from the effects of the alcohol until at last they fell asleep. Porãsy knew the time had come and stealthily approached the entrance to alert her people. But at that very moment, Moñái woke up and pounced on her with a cry of betrayal.

He wrapped his snake body around the young woman and pulled her back into the cave. Porãsy, realizing her salvation was impossible, shouted to her tribe to block the cave's entrance.

Tumê Arandú's men blocked the entrance with a large stone and set fire to the hill to seal the fate of the monsters forever along with that of the brave young woman.

Porãsy's sublime sacrifice to free the land from the cursed monsters will be remembered forever. Tupã, to reward her dedication, raised the heroine's soul to heaven and turned it into a small but intense point of light, which the Guarani tribes call *mbyja ko'ê*.

From that point on, the spirit of Porãsy lights up the sky at dusk and dawn.

Naipi and Taruba

Legend has it that in a village on the banks of the Iguazú River lived a beautiful maiden named Naipi who was to be married to a great warrior named Taruba from a nearby tribe. One day, Naipi went walking along the banks of the river, and as Mbói Tu'ĩ passed along the river he looked up and saw her and he fell in love with her. He decided he must have her and went to the Guaraní elders demanding they give her to him as a sacrifice.

Of course, poor Naipi was frightened and Taruba was determined to save her. They decided to run away together, even though they knew that if Mbói Tu'ĩ found out he would kill them both. Despite the danger, they decided that death together would be better than death apart.

As Naipi and Taruba were setting off in a canoe to escape down the river, the serpent lord saw them and chased after them furiously. Mbói Tu'ĩ became so angry that his serpent body expanded to the width of the river. As he twisted and turned, he created new curves in the river making the canoe rock dangerously, but this only increased the anger and determination of Taruba who rowed even harder, refusing to give up.

Mbói Tu'ĩ became so filled with rage he caused the very earth to split apart and the river to plummet downwards, creating what is now Iguazú Falls. The sheer force sent Taruba flying from the canoe to land on the bank below.

Trapped in the falling canoe, Naipi watched helplessly as the bottom of the chasm opened up underneath her. As she was about to smash into the bottom, Mbói Tu'ĩ transformed her into a massive rock to stop her from escaping him.

On seeing his beloved turn to stone, Taruba attempted to reach her, but as he stretched out his fingers to try and take hold of her they turned into roots and Taruba turned into a palm tree on the Brazilian side of the falls. From this position Taruba could see Naipi on the Argentine side of the falls and she could see him but they could never again touch, kiss or embrace.

To make sure this never happens, the jealous serpent lord watches them from a deep part of the river called the Devil's Throat. Nevertheless, although Naipi and Taruba cannot be reunited, their love can always be seen forming a rainbow from the palm tree on the Brazilian side of the falls to the rock that is Naipi on the Argentine side.

GLOSSARY OF GUARANÍ TERMS

- **mita'i:** child
- **che memby:** my child
- **che membykuña:** my daughter
- **che sy:** my mother
- **che ru:** my father
- **che ra'a:** my friend
- **ñande sy:** our mother

- **y:** water
- **yvy:** earth
- **yvytu:** air
- **yvyty:** mountain
- **y guazú**: big water (waterfall)

- **petei:** one
- **pokoi:** seven
- **kuña:** woman
- **kuña mbareté:** strong woman
- **yaguareté**: jaguar
- **tatakua:** oven (lit. fire hole)
- **yrupé:** water lily
- **pindovy:** palm tree
- **ka'a:** plant

- **ka'aguy:** forest
- **ka'a ruvicha:** king of plants
- **ko'eti:** dawn
- **jaharí gua'a:** macaw, guacamayo
- **arko iris:** rainbow
- **temikuave'e:** sacrifice
- **ñemendápe:** wedding
- **py'aguasu:** courage
- **pyhare:** evening
- **mbyja ko'e:** morning star

Guaraní Expressions:

- **Ma'ena:** What a shame!
- **Che vare'a:** I'm hungry.
- **Ja'umina:** Let's eat!
- **Nde'rasore:** What the hell?
- **Opáma:** It's all done!
- **Ñandejára:** Oh my god!
- **Iporãitereí:** That's good!
- **Ñembosarai:** Let's play!
- **Rohayhu:** I love you

REFERENCES

Colman, Narciso R. (1929). Ñande *Ypy Kuéra*. Asunción, Paraguay.

González Torres, Dionisio M. (1995). *Folclore del Paraguay*. Asunción, Paraguay.

Micó, Tomas L. (1980). *Leyendas y mitos del Paraguay*. Asunción, Paraguay.

ABOUT THE AUTHOR

Clara Elena García (aka C.E. Wallace) is a Paraguayan-born poet and author based in New York. By day, she runs a school for migrant children awaiting reunification with their families in the U.S. By night, she writes, creates, and makes music with her husband and very spoiled cat.

Her first book, "Juego de Palabras," was published in 2023 by Valparaíso Ediciones. Clara's poems have been published in the *Acentos Review*,

Alebrijes Review, *Axon Journal*, *Cuéntame Literary Magazine,* and *Sonic Boom Journal.*

She also has work in five anthologies- *You're Never Too Much- Poems for Every Emotion* from *Macmillan, Boundless 2025* from *The Rio Grande Valley International Poetry Festival, The Multilingual Anthology of the America's Poetry Festival of New York* from *Artepoética Press, The Hyperion* from *End of the World Productions* and *The Dark Side of Purity* from *Band of Bards Comics.*

Clara began writing poetry as a teenager, attending the New England Young Writers Conference at Bread Loaf in 2002. Her poetry spans years and experiences and covers topics such as mental health, belonging, romance, and the metaphysical. More recently, she has been immersed in works based on Paraguayan folklore.

Clara was selected to represent Paraguay in The Americas Poetry Festival of New York, which was held on October 11th - 13th, 2023 at the Cervantes Institute of New York and the Walt Whitman Birthplace Association.

ABOUT THE AUTHOR

More recently, she appeared on a panel with the renowned author Rigoberto Gonzalez and award winning translator Alexis Romay on the importance of Spanish-language poetry and has been a guest on several radio shows in the NYC and NJ area.

You can usually find her lurking on social media as @claraelenadice.

For any inquiries about her work or to book her for an event, please reach out to her agent, Atifa Begom at *Crescent Literary*.

www.ingramcontent.com/pod-product-compliance
Lightning Source LLC
Chambersburg PA
CBHW022040290426
44109CB00014B/927